St. Trigger

St. Trigger

Aaron Coleman

Button Poetry / Exploding Pinecone Press
Minneapolis, Minnesota
2016

Published by Button Poetry / Exploding Pinecone Press
Minneapolis, MN 55403

http://buttonpoetry.com

Cover Design: Nikki Clark

ISBN 978-1-943735-06-8

For Lew

Table of Contents

*The pure products of America
go crazy—*

—William Carlos Williams

Viciousness in Ends

blood and trust   in my mouth
on the ground   sweltering each
swing harder   dizzy still   to protect what?

inside red and black gloves with quarter-
worn knuckles   part of a man   two fists thick
no way to know the stranger   from my

brother's hand – the boxing glove still hot
     past it   sticky hand slipping into –
we refused to go   the fear in our throats –

stuck like meat in our teeth   *and it was good*   and it was
   from one another   and sweat genesis   and took
uncut grass   we laughed   face down

in the yellow   to press each other's necks   like dull blades
and used our forearms – where he breaks
     we laughed   because we swore   a man is born

into each other's sharp backs   point blank
     we shot the metal bb's   we shot
the metal bb's point blank into each other's

sharp backs   because we swore a man is born
where he breaks   we laughed and used
    our forearms like dull blades   to press each other's

necks face down   in the yellow uncut grass   we laughed
    and sweat genesis and took   from one another
and it was good   and it was stuck   like meat

in our teeth the fear   in our throats – we refused
          to go past it   sticky hand slipping
into the boxing glove   still hot from my brother's hand –

no way   to know the stranger part   of a man two fists thick
          with quarter-worn knuckles   inside red and black
gloves to protect what?   each swing harder   dizzy

still   on the ground   sweltering blood   and trust in my mouth

St. Inside and Not

Being tornado, being wind-stuck,
Being swamp-swallowed and forgotten, being
Gangster-gone-ghost. Being leaking
And prohibited. Being rugged
Smirk and gut exposed, stone church
Roof removed, ivy-spindled throat. Being
Forever-far from coasts. Being echo clang and
Shale-sick grease rag. Being trundled down
The conveyor belt the wound wound river being
Time-tight, squeezing and seething
And flooding. Being burnheart and holy
Jelly Roll squall and squalor and
Ma called squaw battered in missing shame-
Laden eyes. Being missed and called family, anchor,
Surname: Gone. Being turned into translation,
Being an altar and a mother praying *God save*
Me in a language I'll never know. Being hands
Held high above head, body blown open. Being
Bit-nickel never trusted, being
Runaway sharecropper castrated, burned
Away in pieces in hand-licked heavy
Envelopes. Being letters scrawled: *you*
Missed a big, fiery one. Wish you were
Here. Being midnight ripped
Off the face of constellation. Being
Rage shattered in the body, before
Each risk: live, let die, follow.

Vestigia

The trees teach me how to break and keep on living. Patience
and nuance and another kind of strength. That kind of life
wrought from water and mineral iron and loss, the perpetual loss
that emanates from underneath tongues, leaves. The hush splayed
across the jungle made of memory. More fearful for its lack
of movement. The sad lusciousness our eyes reason from a world
on pause. Motionless green. What we touch and see, immediate as
steam, then gone, collected. Tense, wet beads full of secrets; how
to make a branch long. Nothing swaying the weight of the trees.

Manmade Shelter Beneath Rupturing Sky

I can't tell you, but you feel it the way you feel
       thunder. The way it speaks rain and beckons
a turning back to manmade shelter beneath

       a rupturing sky, a silent *please* between
men who work to claim each other, blood,
       who are supposed to take, to prove, to dig wide

around what burns and not speak out
       loud about love. Fumes fuse when we
hide words under eaves like bushels of wheat
       and watch the barn burn down

as the rain picks up too late. Boys burn down
       and aim to take the town with them. Flames flick light
into pummeling rain, billow black smoke when they break
       open the cans of tractor grease. You won't let yourself

look away from the burning shed as the structure tears
       down in cindered shards of darkness
in the middle of the storm, the middle of the night.

It is not a question of memory

Frost, inexplicable in a mirror like a river
muting my reflection, I see trembling
southern fields, clouds clotted with
shine. Body, still wet, covered
in cold, where the South hides. I
run water over fear, a descant
for recollection. A slow drip down
this nose, lips, chin, down, through
the shoal of impulse and each
border of this torso, scar-laced hip,
belly, thigh, shin. Beneath. My South
thick with pulse. I'll flux into
history, but first let me fuse
language, anguish, touch; give me time
to settle with what anchors shadow
to this face this morning. My South:
both gulf and border, black highways
stitched and caked with rock salt,
the corpse of a red-tailed hawk, swollen
then frozen in ice, now mid-thaw
in the cattails, a sandbar eclipsed in
the stench of sulfur, and my remaining
barefoot in autumn on a man-made
beach, Lake Michigan, even after the wind
picks up. A dozen monarch butterflies
strewn like candy wrappers in seaweed
washed ashore, somehow so close
to asphalt and fluorescence; an iron
city's core. My stark hand damp,
tracing the warped wooden door, South
still staring back through the asking

mirror, back through the memory
of a trip South I've never taken before.

On Acquiescence

Of Bronze – and Blaze…

We were crossing town again, on the bus. Our point guard who
could never sit still, be stilled, said, *Playin' with my money is like playin'
with my emotions,* between his teeth and leaned into the aisle
mimicking Big Worm's anger we'd watched on TV. My teammate
and I shared more than the same name. All of us slapped seats

with laughter, barely understanding, on the bus crossing town in
ties and slacks, heading to our JV game. After school but before
the game, I had wanted to say, *don't play* to a girl I smiled with
too much in her white-on-white volleyball knee-highs and skin,
down in the empty afterschool classroom, both of us too

silent, looking at each other as if lost in the angles of skin and hips
and dusk. Careful games shrouded in change, wanting. I was never
quite sure about her touch, metal-detecting fingertips seeking
shrapnel. We held something quiet. We crossed town, got off
the bus. Chins up, another contest, away. Rarely smiling. Undressing

and changing into uniform I remembered her hands, put mine
where she put hers on my body. A boy said, *And you know this, man.*
We laughed and talked shit when what we wanted to do was
understand. I remember the fists of the boy with my name when he,
hotheaded and light-

skinned, cut across the court, breakneck toward the white
man hurling slurs from the front row of his son's home
game, 4th quarter, seeing a tall, blonde boy – maybe his –
knocked onto hardwood. The perennial black versus white school
rivalry. When my name streaked toward the bleachers cross town,

reaching for the screaming white man, our black feathers rustled
like midnight peacocks claiming our cage, the polished floor.
We were cross town. We were off the bus. We weren't safe.
Not while playing away or sweat-soaked inside
patent leather Jordan's, toes clenched like talons, cursing

with our bodies under the buzzer's horn, straining to empty
what gets stuck in hands fashioned into weapons that clutch
torsos and throats hummed in muscle, flexed shut. Off
at this distance, I hold less and less noise and more silence.
But what if we are made of this violence?

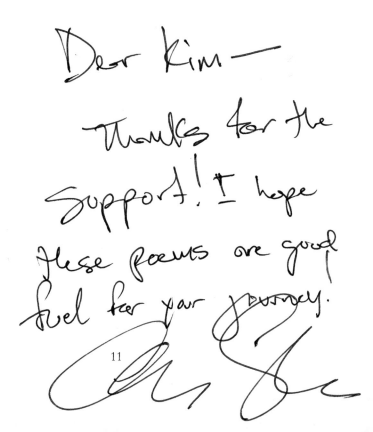

Dear Kim —

Thanks for the
support! I hope
these poems are good
fuel for your journey.

After

I lock a foreign door behind me, leave her
        sleeping. Three days wordless and now
I will not see her more. Her. And will never see

You. By and by. We: fragments of you. And I am made
        by loss. I may never love, hear, and know

the child with the mind I had before. You were us. Now,
        I am made older. Here: Dimly lit

exits and entrances, muted corridors cut
        through an end inside, spiraled blood and dark—
I know a quiet, but don't know who or what

        you were, I am, was. I slowly break a giant
lotus the color of rain cloud with my mouth; stray

        petals, forgiveness, saliva
inept along my lips. Echoes: a shrill woman breaks

        her voice over my body, scowls before she pleads
with the walls I've cobbled into me. A young, tall preacher
        in his prime smiles, mouth closed, and

places faceless coins
        in the deep palm
of my left hand. The bent wire

        grip of the lantern I don't want
creaks sharp in my other hand, thin glass lets go

tattered streams of light, ill sway, insignificance,
absence, beneath raw white sky. This snarl of intuition,
a clutch of sudden roots, believes,

but does not speak. What I remember is everything, but
I know that can't be.

Her Song a Cliff a Cage

How did it end up in that house. Hand-forged
burl and bole and shoulder. Figure sheathed
beneath cloth. What sunk and became
the room. What was draped and standing

taller than this woman who made the woman
who made me known. Restless wire sacrament.
A hole made of music comes wide, inhuman from
a crooked instrument, a torso almost hollowed,
rimmed in shades of pink and ivory. Nothing

black about this anchor. Beyond memory, she touched
its strings, spilled improbable sound. I will
always be a child to that harp. Confused.
Never allowed to touch. A deafening gleam when
its music moved through lightless rooms, through

walls and bodies alike. I became silence. I've become
cumbersome as love I cannot hold. Then let me be
that music that consumes midnight. Let me make
chords with what comes from this blood.

Rich

rich (→) **adj. 1.** Having abundant possessions and especially material wealth: As in, standing a breath between each other, she didn't realize how *rich* she was until she saw him weigh her past in his eyes. **2. a.** Having great worth or value: Remnants of his mother's voice echoed beneath their praise, inside his spine: we may have enough but we ain't *rich*, at least not like them; don't forget your hands are broken mirrors, how they splinter money-colored clouds. **b.** Made of or containing valuable materials: It wasn't their new world's prospects that changed them: they'd become *rich* with what they'd lost, and because of what they were losing; you could tell by the way it swayed their frames, curved their minds. **3.** Magnificently impressive, sumptuous: Despite the flitting birds of his new money and tongue, his deftly rearranging mind, it was true she was the *rich* one; he forced himself to keep his gaze above the ground, open on her eyes. **4. a.** Vivid and deep in color: They were the *rich* amber of dark honey unbecoming itself in green tea. **b.** Full and mellow in tone and quality: She only hesitates because the touch of his voice feels *rich* as music at the edge of her body, *rich* enough to coax home a ghost. **c.** Having a strong fragrance: Her *rich* scent carries something with it, or in it, not only her but something coming through her, running. **5.** Highly productive or remunerative: Their gods said, what you share won't make you *rich*; what will you do with the coin of your lives? **6. a.** Having abundant plant nutrients: They buried their gods in *rich* soil, then searched for months on hands and knees for warmth radiating from the surface, eager to reap the unwild. **b.** Highly seasoned, fatty, oily, or sweet: Their myths, their histories, their pleas, their systems of conviction and logic; they were too *rich* to not be poison. **c.** High in the combustible component: As in, beyond their own *rich* bodies, they could sense a hiss coming low, too, from their world, willing to explode. **d.** High in any component: So they grew, or swelled, guilt-*rich*, shame-*rich*, and ever-teetering at the cusp of knowing so. **7.** Highly varied, developed, or complex: It was the simultaneous intimacy and distance, the real and unreal sense of their lives, their relationships, their auspices that felt so *rich*: so profoundly yet elusively interwoven. **8. a.** Entertaining; also: laughable: But there is something *rich* here; even—or especially—for them, bearing witness to the near emptiness, the falling. **b.** Meaningful, significant: As in, something *rich* enough to let slip less and less slowly. **c.** Lush: She said, you know, the same way a certain, pluraled pain is *rich*. Yes, he added, or a certain pluraled crisis. **9.** Pure or nearly pure: Though they thought they were, they were not *rich* enough to go.

after A. Van Jordan

Sta. Soledad

Especie de dios, que no me toques donde me queda
    The crescent ache that meets the light
    And blinds my failing eyes that work
Crisis, aun voluptuosa, en contra de cada cuchilla de momento,
    cada década de
        Desire tumbled down, ripe with what I won't admit I love

        Each prayer of breath and touch sliced open not enough
Cuando nos dejamos extinguidos, más torcidos que juntos, pero así
    fieles
        To the black hole heart not greedy not lonely
        Only doing what it is supposed to do: claiming
Como la material que somos, hinchada con Gracia, llena del fin
    tanto como lo abierto

Where We Choose to Hide

It was   absolute. It was gorgeous.   *Stay.*

But gorgeous. *Trust.* The cold   bending. The light
from the cathedral. Snow in   our lies. The frost—

seething. Slowly, slowly into summer. How we were

                wrongheaded and heavy with music:
its strange weight. Pulsing, heart-like.

Loss-like. The brutal conviction of seasons.
Blunt nakedness.   Sweat-lush

5100 blocks south.   Dusk-swept, swallowed in
skyline. If not   a horizon. *We can't—*

your eyes. Lake dark, wide
                        windows left open

to dying daylight.   Humid light. Foolish light.
11 floors up.   Weeping.   *Trust. Trust*

this.   We still don't.   Give
a secret to a being. Each

collapsed. Complete. Fever made   of touch.

God's Island

Then a man is a place;
a room cluttered full of walls
within walls, wants within
wants, windows within
windows, mirrors and more
mirrors long and home
enough with hidden sharpness
to catch and reflect each
and every act without seeing,
without making even
the slightest shattering sound.

On Forgiveness

I am a half question seeping into cracked ice
       leaning over the bar's worn wood. Fear
weighted with ache, anxious in the fleshed
       angles of two faces. Slurred symmetry in me
and my old man's shadow when he cackles.
       Saliva and vodka flick embers working
fire into my skin. No one else sees the sway
       and lean in his bulk, the terror coarse
in his veins. His loose hands touch slick,
       wet glass; a promise of sharpness. Don't
murmur *I love you,* this time. Don't
       come close. Give me the keys and shut
the fuck up if I swerve in the dark
       summer heat by the swamp
land you taught me to own.

Through

through (→) **prep. 1.** In one side and out the opposite or another side of: As in, after days of wandering, they finally carved a path *through* the deep woods; the littlest of them all couldn't help but stare at how the standing water had soaked *through* his socks. When he opened his mouth to speak, the bigger ones looked right *through* him and continued forward toward the cave's mouth. **2.** Among or between; in the midst of: She watched him gently as he fell *through* his mind. They chose silence because the sound of their fear travelled so clumsily *through* darkness. **3.** By way of: *Through* sex, they spilled loss and time. *Through* sex, they learned to desire their most intimate disguises. **4. a.** By the means or agency of: She learned how to distinguish between different kinds of smiles *through* her trips to the general store with her mother, grandmother, and later on *through* her daughter. **b.** Into and out of the handling, care, processing, modification, or consideration of: They shuffled his application *through* the unemployment office at the same speed he went *through* each job. His stint on the steamboat casino was his favorite; he remembered the first moment the chips no longer felt like money, the way colors began to blur, passing *through* his hands like the gray chaos of river water. **5.** Here and there in; around: He was sure there was something else speaking *through* his veins besides blood. As they walked *through* the antebellum home, he couldn't believe the way the smells forced their way *through* his clothes, his skin, his nostrils; the staining scent of cigar, the musk of sweat and shame, the lingering hints of salt pork, sweet corn, and gun powder. **6.** From the beginning to the end of: *Through* it all, he had known deep down that he had never wanted to be there. He didn't know why he stayed *through* the rumblings and *through* the shatter; why didn't he just say he had to go? He lay there *through* the night, eyes open, mouth closed. **7.** At or to the end of; done or finished with, especially successfully: They were relieved to be *through* each phase of pain. They were *through* with every claim except exhaustion. **8.** Up to and including: They went *through* the first eleven pages of the manifest without finding his name and he watched the man's eyes as he scanned *through* the last one. She had gone *through* all her options; there appeared to be no way out. **9.** Past and without stopping for: For years, they touched and moved smoothly *through* only the bodies they didn't love; together they devised a plan and plot to get *through* the smaller deaths and desires. **10.** Because of; on account of: She thought she could manage to survive *through* silence. He was sure that he could survive long enough *through* some combination of his grip and his feet.

after A. Van Jordan

Between

bliss and fear. I learn the waves before

the tides. Toes skimming the bottom,
what I do remember is
her farther out, in

the bigger waves and her body held

beyond, above my head in the swell—
the inrushing water, for a moment
a silhouette, a threat, dissolving, nearly

bodiless, riding, rising—turquoise light,
that is what the guilt is like.

Wherein I am

mostly in my palms
    shoved deep in pockets full of red

dirt and tattered psalms pressed into skin
    inside a threaded edge
        around my waist
   stricken
          strained

*

a greased piston
    of a vehicle   passing

the asphalt beneath
   the driver's hand
      slipping

from the wheel
    succumbing to sleep

*

confined to a theater fearing
   bullets on repeat
      watching every motion

picture I was supposed to watch
    only years too late

   with acetate film meant to protect

              my pupils
                 translucent
dripping

                     anxious blue

              *

       beetle-backed
            exo-
                 and gossamer-winged
          spreading
open until too far
       until torn down the middle
                     until clouded
                             viscera splaying
          exposed

       *

moonlight extended
                over an open
          field in southern Illinois
                             its southing
I am also
          the corn sheathed
                     nearby
             its husk
   shimmering in white light

27

St. Seduction

Eros eating my eyes, full-mouth rosy
smile ever so slightly   righteous—
        drooling. I do with my myths what they do
with me. I do not believe.   I choose to eat
          my way through dark   bridges. I swallow
idle gods. Yours? Whose? They dance
        they sex they hand they look they gut
whatever whoever: all and only
          to distort   the way I stilt and syncopate
through time's violence. Distinguish me
        from night   that lives inside you.
The myth: of me. The want   to want
          to be. Wanted. Sacred. Silent. Magnetic—how
so hollowed by light. Maze of
          body. Wracked with pulse and touch. Curve
and arc and eye. Again. Quick. Smile.
          The guilt of whom   I—we—you aren't
throbbing. I spy the wild bedrooms in bodies
          porous with instinct. Smell. Orgiastic loss
grasps—conspires. The ache
          of expiration—exploration. Look. At me
through them in us, restless foot dangling
          off the curb over the puddle into the glance
of the other—there—upside down inside
          you falling. Up. Rushing where with whom and why
ecstatic and hazed   delicious light   caught
          lost falling. Loot   loot—Look through
into— my face is not a door my face
          is not a door my face my—   as if the truth were
most important. And it, I, too, seduce
          the same way warm sea rises higher

by the hour. I do not believe
in righteousness. Such lonely power.

On Surrender

The soft dark rope of prayer and dream,
its weight, what I pull, and am pulled by
into night. Crude apparatus. I walked into what seemed

to be a wake in the ordering line
of a 24-hour McDonald's downtown. I was camouflage
contraband, everything I looked at looked back

black and white. From my peripheral, I witnessed
my counterfeit life: the only police
officer I've ever trusted, an ex-lover,
a savior, a martyr, a brother, all there

waiting: worldless, anxious, hungry – so many leaned
their shadows on each other. Someone I knew once
spoke aloud to no one: Who broke me open?

The nightwind and what it carried made it hard
to know. Time was a threat we noticed so
I gave in to slow sex that felt like a memory,
got zip-tied by that police officer, then haphazardly
released. I never got my food.

                              White people
I vaguely recognized talked shit about Detroit
comfortable between the cramped
bathroom's piss and stone and I felt
myself swell to defend a city within
whose limits I've never lived. I'm ashamed
I don't trust anger. I'm ashamed I don't trust
the idea of home. Outside, I saw the war

again. I wanted
to sit on the floor, sit until I was served, and eat, but I knew
nothing, no one, would come. Until too late, our bodies
couldn't grasp the incoming weary glory of the out-of-date
military drones, gunning at us, until they were less
than the height of an abandoned tenement above
the ground tattered with violence, spitting up
crumbles. Before anything else: the numbness

of this danger, this power. We pushed
each other into the parking lot's narrow
sorrow and threw hand-size chunks of rock

into the sky, and hated the way the child-like
among us paused in awe of the destruction.
You are less if you miss, we'd say. *Keep fucking throwing.*
Each one of us, on our own, gave up. I went back

inside to find someone I still love. The two of us rushed
to stash our bodies together in condiment cupboards
beneath the cash register. We made ourselves pray
but my knees wouldn't bend enough

to close the little door, so I left her there. Went back again
and pressed my hand on the glass
exit, took in the sudden emptiness, and felt the toll
stir my body, full, and hopeless.

Seed Beneath The Dark

The fretwork breaks. The sanctuary abandoned, burns
up through the ends of stars. I name each blamed
forest Today and Why and Year and Gone. Trust
the wolf, the owl, the crag, the lip of rock above
the vulture that murmurs *look*. I counted. I took.
I wove myself in with the leaves. My fortune refused
to surprise me. Thought, then forgetfulness – what if
I believe fear is its own low country? I know
an hour behind an hour and the tower inside
an elegy. I am anybody helpless, listless, near
as whisper, as prayer. There is a quiet inside every
valley and door. I build hundreds of my own angels
and dare the cold to mold me daily into a bridge
between what I have forgotten and what I owe.

Elegy for Apogee

Drowning? Consider this: What is desire? Who or what devours
what or whom? How close is absurdity, is irrelevance, is danger?
In denial? In the divine? In dilated eyes? In sunken hands
scrubbing pans in the kitchen that cooks hunger beneath fish-
greased dish water? What is that tremble in the feet and the mouth
of the fly romancing the crumbs on the brim of the sink
from the night before? Do we have to eat everything? Do we have
to chew endlessly and never burn our tongues or choke

gobbling soup or razor-thin hidden bones? This deliciousness
still too hot? Too piercing to the throat? Can you choke her
if she asks you to squeeze hard no harder no keep going but don't
enjoy it too much? Do we have to lust for nights fucking fucking
otherness until we hear the clink of new armor gleaming
sweat-polished and mooned by breath turned noise? Can we lie
there in our sex exhausted and still swallow and still remain
touched, halved, inside, conscious of conscience? Whose

conscience? Whose collateral? Whose collapse? Whose end? Who's
dark as the id? Breed the id? Eat the id? Be exotic to myself? Enjoy
the translation of my body in whose mouth? Who can work
with hurt and urge and rage like words, like puzzles,
like bodies, like whose? Bring out which tantalizing bodies
from the stockroom and wild reserve of my own? Pile platters high
with meat and cheese cultured and aged in the skin of a what? Cut

it how? Watch for what to gush? Spread it how? How much of this
mind is mine? Where is my canary? Who has the brand new one-
size-fits-all jumpsuit and boots, the helmet with its dim light barely
carrying? And what should we do with the soot seeping into the
porous pornography of my taboo-being giving up? Who owns

the other wild canaries kidnapped from their islands for cages
of coal-fraught mines? Who can explain what happened? Dondé

estaban? Y dondé estoy? Como vas ahora negrito? Negrita? Como
andas adentro conquistador sin doors? What did you ever love
enough to try to take, to force open, to touch, conquistador?
Disfrutas de deseo tanto como dices? Do you hate as much as you
say you hate? What about the tired yellow disappearing from all
these delicate feathers? How long do we have to wait
to coat our quills with kindling before we explode? Forget
my ancestral antique cave? Forget my myths? Forget my holes?

What about the spilling-in cold? Where's the hair? Where's the bulk?
Who's been shorn? I am on display as owned bones in what
museum-made-home? What want won't leave me alone?
Why and how do bodies fuck and war, pattern and rattle
the windows in the ecstatic upper rooms of the special collections
gallery? Who can say they love the ache of their anger?
Who can really say they trust anger the way they trust want? Who
doesn't ask? Who's anxious? Who's anchored to the brutal arc

inside of eyes? To drunk fumbling hands atop the antique dining
room table? To the loll of heirloom lace? To felt green worn
corners on whose pool table? To the sacrosanct crawl
space? To the naked hangers clattering in whose closet?
To the craters of the body's moonscape movie set backed
by big-time producers of what reeling nostalgia? To which actors
delivering breakthrough after breakthrough performance after
performance? To which decrepit theater of my body, collapsed

and taken back by the roots and vines of trees,
an abandoned stage dim and splintered with what kind of want?

[American Dream] See

two black people [what] in an alley naked
[am i] having sex frantic in a cop car
with the cop lights chaotic [silent?] circling
across the walls [what]. See two black

people in an alley naked having
sex in a cop car cop lights writ frantic [am i]
across the walls [gone]. The sirens fracture
shadows, whir, near – unsilent [?] – drawn.

St. Trigger

I'm idolized

      taboo   I'm   backhanded eye

          who holds you   backward

close like fire   in myself

                I'm split   heat spilt

I'm no   thing   but   from human   ripped

    new   to you   I'm wire   void and nova   loosed

      soaked   cloaked   I'm scar

        in   anti-antidote   I'm   contrived

            hole   in hope   wind   antennae

I'm end   of obsolescent sex   looped—   meant to be

    pressed   marked man   slewed   transmitted

        beneath   ruthless   music—

I'm   a ready finger   I'm admission and

a ready thumb—

ambitious suspicion

derision

I'm   unclocked time   I'm hum
and tick   and boom
hymn
doubled
lobbed brick   daemoned   delicious decision
look
spewed into   Pantocrator   devoured   attended
the truth   I'm   symptom   religioned
I'm sum   man-i-fold masque
of angels   afraid   fate-taken
I'm debt   made   face-stricken
I'm learned   ache   ace   I'm   what happens
burn   and want   divided   born
and doubt adept   ashamed   I'm rabid
I've had it   aimed   aped—

Notes

The title "It is not a question of memory" quotes James Baldwin's essay "Many Thousands Gone," from his collection of essays, *Notes of a Native Son.*

The epigraph of "On Acquiescence" refers to Emily Dickinson's "Of Bronze – and Blaze." The italicized language in the poem quotes the characters Big Worm and Smokey in the 1995 movie, Friday.

"Rich" and "Through" owe their dictionary form to several poems in A. Van Jordan's collection *M-A-C-N-O-L-I-A.*

The title and beginning of the first line of "Between" are drawn from part of a sentence in James Weldon Johnson's *The Autobiography of an Ex-Colored Man*: "The anticipation produced in me a sensation somewhat between bliss and fear."

Acknowledgments

I'd like to extend my gratitude and appreciation to the following journals and anthology in which poems in this chapbook (or previous versions of them) first appeared: *Apogee, Bettering American Poetry, Button Poetry, The Greensboro Review, Meridian, Pinwheel, River Styx, Southern Indiana Review, Third Coast,* and *Tupelo Quarterly.*

To my parents and my whole family, for who they are; for their indomitable love and support, their grace and their complications.
To my GBC fam (homegrown and those who came), Tiffany, Mithil, and to Andrea for what we're creating, and for lifting me up.

For so many years of guidance, insight, and friendship, Diane Seuss. For believing in me and opening my eyes even further, Jericho Brown. For the growth you spark and who you are, Mary Jo Bang and Carl Phillips.

I offer my thanks and appreciation to the communities of the Creative Writing Program and the Chancellor's Graduate Fellowship Program at Washington University in St. Louis for their unique and essential support: social, emotional, and financial. Thank you to Cave Canem, for our faith, resilience, what we're building, and how we're growing. In addition to those named above, I would be remiss without extending special thanks to Espelencia Baptiste, VersAnnette Blackman-Bosia, rebecca brown, Kathryn Davis, Timothy Donnelly, Danielle Dutton, Kathleen Finneran, Rav Grewal-Kok, Saskia Hamilton, Kathryn A. Hindenlang, francine j. harris, Jennifer Kronovet, Paul Legault, Liz London, Miriam Martínez, Philip Matthews, William J. Maxwell, Charleen McClure, Michael Mlekoday (Thanks, Editor!), Sope Oyelaran, Vivian Pollak, Katie Prout, Claudia Rankine, Justin Phillip Reed, Line Rindvig, Mónica de la Torre, Phillip B. Williams, Eileen Wilson-Oyelaran, Rafia Zafar, and Pablo Zavala. Thank you, too, to all the other friends and artists, too many to name here (I see you), that have offered insights and encouragement along the way.

I offer my heartfelt gratitude to the communities of educators, writers, and young people in Madrid, Spain, Durban, South Africa, and Chicago, Illinois, whose influences will resonate with me as long as I am. Thank you to the Fulbright Program, the Beeler Fellowship at Kalamazoo College, and Literature for All of Us, respectively, for their financial support in those endeavors.

And thank you, Adrian Matejka, for seeing potential in this chapbook.

About the Author

A Fulbright Scholar and Cave Canem Fellow from Metro-Detroit, Aaron Coleman has lived and worked with youth in locations including Kalamazoo, Chicago, Spain, and South Africa. A graduate of Washington University in St. Louis' MFA Program and Kalamazoo College in Psychology, Aaron most recently taught Poetry Writing at Washington University in St. Louis, worked as Public Projects Assistant at Pulitzer Arts Foundation, and was co-poetry editor for *The Spectacle*. His poems have recently appeared or are forthcoming in *Apogee, Boston Review, Fence, The Greensboro Review, Meridian, Pinwheel, River Styx, Southern Indiana Review, Third Coast, Tupelo Quarterly*, and elsewhere. A two-time semifinalist for the 92Y Discovery Poetry Contest and winner of the Tupelo Quarterly TQ5 Poetry Contest, Aaron is currently a PhD student in Washington University in St. Louis' Comparative Literature Program, where he is studying translation.

Other Books by Button Poetry

Aziza Barnes, *me Aunt Jemima and the nailgun.*

J. Scott Brownlee, *Highway or Belief*

Sam Sax, *A Guide to Undressing Your Monsters*

Nate Marshall, *Blood Percussion*

Mahogany L. Browne, *smudge*

Neil Hilborn, *Our Numbered Days*

Sierra DeMulder, *We Slept Here*

Danez Smith, *Black Movie*

Cameron Awkward-Rich, *Transit*

Jacqui Germain, *When the Ghosts Come Ashore*

Hanif Willis-Abdurraqib, *The Crown Ain't Worth Much*